Date:_____

Daily Positive Thought

Daily Goal

_____

_____

Action Plan

6am	
7am	
8am	
9am	
10am	
11am	
12pm	
1pm	
2pm	
3pm	
4pm	
5pm	
6pm	
7pm	
8pm	

To-Do List

Top Priority
- ❑
- ❑
- ❑

Needs doing
- ❑
- ❑
- ❑

Low Priority
- ❑
- ❑

Today I Feel

I have the power to

I deal with challenges by

What went well today?

What could have gone better?

What will tomorrow bring for you?

Ideas, Thoughts and Doodles

Date:_____

Daily Positive Thought

_____

_____

Daily Goal

To-Do List

Top Priority

❑

❑

❑

Needs doing

❑

❑

❑

Low Priority

❑

❑

Action Plan

6am	
7am	
8am	
9am	
10am	
11am	
12pm	
1pm	
2pm	
3pm	
4pm	
5pm	
6pm	
7pm	
8pm	

Today I Feel

I have the power to

I deal with challenges by

What went well today?

What could have gone better?

What will tomorrow bring for you?

Ideas, Thoughts and Doodles

Date:_____

Daily Positive Thought

Daily Goal

To-Do List

Top Priority

❑

❑

❑

Needs doing

❑

❑

❑

Low Priority

❑

❑

Action Plan

6am	
7am	
8am	
9am	
10am	
11am	
12pm	
1pm	
2pm	
3pm	
4pm	
5pm	
6pm	
7pm	
8pm	

Today I Feel

I have the power to

I deal with challenges by

What went well today?

What could have gone better?

What will tomorrow bring for you?

Ideas, Thoughts and Doodles

Date:_____

Daily Positive Thought

Daily Goal

_____

_____

_____

Action Plan

6am	
7am	
8am	
9am	
10am	
11am	
12pm	
1pm	
2pm	
3pm	
4pm	
5pm	
6pm	
7pm	
8pm	

To-Do List

Top Priority

❑

❑

❑

Needs doing

❑

❑

❑

Low Priority

❑

❑

Today I Feel

I deal with challenges by

I have the power to

What went well today?

What could have gone better?

What will tomorrow bring for you?

Ideas, Thoughts and Doodles

Date:_____

Daily Positive Thought

_____
_____
_____

Daily Goal

Action Plan

| 6am |
| 7am |
| 8am |
| 9am |
| 10am |
| 11am |
| 12pm |
| 1pm |
| 2pm |
| 3pm |
| 4pm |
| 5pm |
| 6pm |
| 7pm |
| 8pm |

To-Do List

Top Priority
❑

❑

❑

Needs doing
❑

❑

❑

Low Priority
❑

❑

Today I Feel

I have the power to

I deal with challenges by

What went well today?

What could have gone better?

What will tomorrow bring for you?

Ideas, Thoughts and Doodles

Date:_____

Daily Positive Thought

_____
_____
_____

Daily Goal

To-Do List

Top Priority

❑

❑

❑

Needs doing

❑

❑

❑

Low Priority

❑

❑

Action Plan

6am	
7am	
8am	
9am	
10am	
11am	
12pm	
1pm	
2pm	
3pm	
4pm	
5pm	
6pm	
7pm	
8pm	

Today I Feel

I deal with challenges by

I have the power to

What went well today?

What could have gone better?

What will tomorrow bring for you?

Ideas, Thoughts and Doodles

Date:_____

Daily Positive Thought

Daily Goal

To-Do List

Top Priority
- ☐
- ☐
- ☐

Needs doing
- ☐
- ☐
- ☐

Low Priority
- ☐
- ☐

Today I Feel

I have the power to

Action Plan

6am
7am
8am
9am
10am
11am
12pm
1pm
2pm
3pm
4pm
5pm
6pm
7pm
8pm

I deal with challenges by

What went well today?

What could have gone better?

What will tomorrow bring for you?

Ideas, Thoughts and Doodles

Date:_____

Daily Positive Thought

_____
_____
_____

Daily Goal

To-Do List

Top Priority

☐

☐

☐

Needs doing

☐

☐

☐

Low Priority

☐

☐

Today I Feel

I have the power to

Action Plan

6am	
7am	
8am	
9am	
10am	
11am	
12pm	
1pm	
2pm	
3pm	
4pm	
5pm	
6pm	
7pm	
8pm	

I deal with challenges by

What went well today?

What could have gone better?

What will tomorrow bring for you?

Ideas, Thoughts and Doodles

Date:_____

Daily Positive Thought

_____
_____
_____

Daily Goal

Action Plan

6am

7am

8am

9am

10am

11am

12pm

1pm

2pm

3pm

4pm

5pm

6pm

7pm

8pm

To-Do List

Top Priority

☐

☐

☐

Needs doing

☐

☐

☐

Low Priority

☐

☐

Today I Feel

I deal with challenges by

I have the power to

What went well today?

What could have gone better?

What will tomorrow bring for you?

Ideas, Thoughts and Doodles

Date:_____

Daily Positive Thought

Daily Goal

_____

_____

To-Do List

Action Plan

Top Priority

❑

❑

❑

Needs doing

❑

❑

❑

Low Priority

❑

❑

6am	
7am	
8am	
9am	
10am	
11am	
12pm	
1pm	
2pm	
3pm	
4pm	
5pm	
6pm	
7pm	
8pm	

Today I Feel

I deal with challenges by

I have the power to

What went well today?

What could have gone better?

What will tomorrow bring for you?

Ideas, Thoughts and Doodles

Date: _____

Daily Positive Thought

_____

_____

_____

Daily Goal

Action Plan

6am

7am

8am

9am

10am

11am

12pm

1pm

2pm

3pm

4pm

5pm

6pm

7pm

8pm

To-Do List

Top Priority

❑

❑

❑

Needs doing

❑

❑

❑

Low Priority

❑

❑

Today I Feel

I deal with challenges by

I have the power to

What went well today?

What could have gone better?

What will tomorrow bring for you?

Ideas, Thoughts and Doodles

Date:_____

Daily Positive Thought

_____

_____

Daily Goal

To-Do List

Top Priority
☐

☐

☐

Needs doing
☐

☐

☐

Low Priority
☐

☐

Action Plan

6am	
7am	
8am	
9am	
10am	
11am	
12pm	
1pm	
2pm	
3pm	
4pm	
5pm	
6pm	
7pm	
8pm	

Today I Feel

I deal with challenges by

I have the power to

What went well today?

What could have gone better?

What will tomorrow bring for you?

Ideas, Thoughts and Doodles

Date:_____

Daily Positive Thought

Daily Goal

_____
_____
_____

To-Do List

Top Priority

☐

☐

☐

Needs doing

☐

☐

☐

Low Priority

☐

☐

Action Plan

6am

7am

8am

9am

10am

11am

12pm

1pm

2pm

3pm

4pm

5pm

6pm

7pm

8pm

Today I Feel

I have the power to

I deal with challenges by

What went well today?

What could have gone better?

What will tomorrow bring for you?

Ideas, Thoughts and Doodles

Date:_____

Daily Positive Thought

_____

_____

Daily Goal

To-Do List

Top Priority

☐

☐

☐

Needs doing

☐

☐

☐

Low Priority

☐

☐

Action Plan

6am	
7am	
8am	
9am	
10am	
11am	
12pm	
1pm	
2pm	
3pm	
4pm	
5pm	
6pm	
7pm	
8pm	

Today I Feel

I have the power to

I deal with challenges by

What went well today?

What could have gone better?

What will tomorrow bring for you?

Ideas, Thoughts and Doodles

Date:_____

Daily Positive Thought

_____

_____

_____

Daily Goal

To-Do List

Top Priority

☐

☐

☐

Needs doing

☐

☐

☐

Low Priority

☐

☐

Action Plan

6am

7am

8am

9am

10am

11am

12pm

1pm

2pm

3pm

4pm

5pm

6pm

7pm

8pm

Today I Feel

I have the power to

I deal with challenges by

What went well today?

What could have gone better?

What will tomorrow bring for you?

Ideas, Thoughts and Doodles

Date:_____

Daily Positive Thought

Daily Goal

_____
_____
_____

To-Do List

Top Priority

☐

☐

☐

Needs doing

☐

☐

☐

Low Priority

☐

☐

Action Plan

6am
7am
8am
9am
10am
11am
12pm
1pm
2pm
3pm
4pm
5pm
6pm
7pm
8pm

Today I Feel

I have the power to

I deal with challenges by

What went well today?

What could have gone better?

What will tomorrow bring for you?

Ideas, Thoughts and Doodles

Date:_____

Daily Positive Thought

_____
_____
_____

Daily Goal

Action Plan

6am	
7am	
8am	
9am	
10am	
11am	
12pm	
1pm	
2pm	
3pm	
4pm	
5pm	
6pm	
7pm	
8pm	

To-Do List

Top Priority
❑

❑

❑

Needs doing
❑

❑

❑

Low Priority
❑

❑

Today I Feel

I have the power to

I deal with challenges by

What went well today?

What could have gone better?

What will tomorrow bring for you?

Ideas, Thoughts and Doodles

Date:_____

Daily Positive Thought

_____
_____
_____

Daily Goal

To-Do List

Top Priority

☐

☐

☐

Needs doing

☐

☐

☐

Low Priority

☐

☐

Action Plan

6am

7am

8am

9am

10am

11am

12pm

1pm

2pm

3pm

4pm

5pm

6pm

7pm

8pm

Today I Feel

I have the power to

I deal with challenges by

What went well today?

What could have gone better?

What will tomorrow bring for you?

Ideas, Thoughts and Doodles

Date:_____

Daily Positive Thought

_____
_____
_____

Daily Goal

To-Do List

Top Priority

❑

❑

❑

Needs doing

❑

❑

❑

Low Priority

❑

❑

Action Plan

6am	
7am	
8am	
9am	
10am	
11am	
12pm	
1pm	
2pm	
3pm	
4pm	
5pm	
6pm	
7pm	
8pm	

Today I Feel

I have the power to

I deal with challenges by

What went well today?

What could have gone better?

What will tomorrow bring for you?

Ideas, Thoughts and Doodles

Date:_____

Daily Positive Thought

_____

_____

Daily Goal

To-Do List

Top Priority

☐

☐

☐

Needs doing

☐

☐

☐

Low Priority

☐

☐

Action Plan

6am

7am

8am

9am

10am

11am

12pm

1pm

2pm

3pm

4pm

5pm

6pm

7pm

8pm

Today I Feel

I deal with challenges by

I have the power to

What went well today?

What could have gone better?

What will tomorrow bring for you?

Ideas, Thoughts and Doodles

Date:_____

Daily Positive Thought

_____

_____

Daily Goal

To-Do List

Top Priority

☐

☐

☐

Needs doing

☐

☐

☐

Low Priority

☐

☐

Action Plan

| 6am |
| 7am |
| 8am |
| 9am |
| 10am |
| 11am |
| 12pm |
| 1pm |
| 2pm |
| 3pm |
| 4pm |
| 5pm |
| 6pm |
| 7pm |
| 8pm |

Today I Feel

I have the power to

I deal with challenges by

What went well today?

What could have gone better?

What will tomorrow bring for you?

Ideas, Thoughts and Doodles

Date:_____

Daily Positive Thought

_____
_____
_____

Daily Goal

To-Do List

Top Priority
❑

❑

❑

Needs doing
❑

❑

❑

Low Priority
❑

❑

Action Plan

6am	
7am	
8am	
9am	
10am	
11am	
12pm	
1pm	
2pm	
3pm	
4pm	
5pm	
6pm	
7pm	
8pm	

Today I Feel

I deal with challenges by

I have the power to

What went well today?

What could have gone better?

What will tomorrow bring for you?

Ideas, Thoughts and Doodles

Date:_____

Daily Positive Thought

Daily Goal

To-Do List

Top Priority

☐

☐

☐

Needs doing

☐

☐

☐

Low Priority

☐

☐

Action Plan

6am

7am

8am

9am

10am

11am

12pm

1pm

2pm

3pm

4pm

5pm

6pm

7pm

8pm

Today I Feel

I have the power to

I deal with challenges by

What went well today?

What could have gone better?

What will tomorrow bring for you?

Ideas, Thoughts and Doodles

Date:_____

Daily Positive Thought

_____

_____

Daily Goal

To-Do List

Top Priority

☐

☐

☐

Needs doing

☐

☐

☐

Low Priority

☐

☐

Action Plan

6am

7am

8am

9am

10am

11am

12pm

1pm

2pm

3pm

4pm

5pm

6pm

7pm

8pm

Today I Feel

I have the power to

I deal with challenges by

What went well today?

What could have gone better?

What will tomorrow bring for you?

Ideas, Thoughts and Doodles

Date:_____

Daily Positive Thought

_____

_____

Daily Goal

To-Do List

Top Priority

❑

❑

❑

Needs doing

❑

❑

❑

Low Priority

❑

❑

Action Plan

6am	
7am	
8am	
9am	
10am	
11am	
12pm	
1pm	
2pm	
3pm	
4pm	
5pm	
6pm	
7pm	
8pm	

Today I Feel

I have the power to

I deal with challenges by

What went well today?

What could have gone better?

What will tomorrow bring for you?

Ideas, Thoughts and Doodles

Date:_____

Daily Positive Thought

_____
_____
_____

Daily Goal

To-Do List

Top Priority

☐

☐

☐

Needs doing

☐

☐

☐

Low Priority

☐

☐

Action Plan

6am	
7am	
8am	
9am	
10am	
11am	
12pm	
1pm	
2pm	
3pm	
4pm	
5pm	
6pm	
7pm	
8pm	

Today I Feel

I deal with challenges by

I have the power to

What went well today?

What could have gone better?

What will tomorrow bring for you?

Ideas, Thoughts and Doodles

Date:_____

Daily Positive Thought

_____
_____
_____

Daily Goal

To-Do List

Top Priority
- ☐
- ☐
- ☐

Needs doing
- ☐
- ☐
- ☐

Low Priority
- ☐
- ☐

Action Plan

6am	
7am	
8am	
9am	
10am	
11am	
12pm	
1pm	
2pm	
3pm	
4pm	
5pm	
6pm	
7pm	
8pm	

Today I Feel

I have the power to

I deal with challenges by

What went well today?

What could have gone better?

What will tomorrow bring for you?

Ideas, Thoughts and Doodles

Date:_____

Daily Positive Thought

_____
_____
_____

Daily Goal

To-Do List

Top Priority

☐

☐

☐

Needs doing

☐

☐

☐

Low Priority

☐

☐

Action Plan

6am

7am

8am

9am

10am

11am

12pm

1pm

2pm

3pm

4pm

5pm

6pm

7pm

8pm

Today I Feel

I have the power to

I deal with challenges by

What went well today?

What could have gone better?

What will tomorrow bring for you?

Ideas, Thoughts and Doodles

Date:_____

Daily Positive Thought

_____
_____
_____

Daily Goal

Action Plan

6am	
7am	
8am	
9am	
10am	
11am	
12pm	
1pm	
2pm	
3pm	
4pm	
5pm	
6pm	
7pm	
8pm	

To-Do List

Top Priority

☐

☐

☐

Needs doing

☐

☐

☐

Low Priority

☐

☐

Today I Feel

I deal with challenges by

I have the power to

What went well today?

What could have gone better?

What will tomorrow bring for you?

Ideas, Thoughts and Doodles

Date:_____

Daily Positive Thought

_____
_____
_____

Daily Goal

To-Do List

Top Priority

☐

☐

☐

Needs doing

☐

☐

☐

Low Priority

☐

☐

Action Plan

6am

7am

8am

9am

10am

11am

12pm

1pm

2pm

3pm

4pm

5pm

6pm

7pm

8pm

Today I Feel

I deal with challenges by

I have the power to

What went well today?

What could have gone better?

What will tomorrow bring for you?

Ideas, Thoughts and Doodles

Date:_____

Daily Positive Thought

_____

_____

Daily Goal

To-Do List

Top Priority
- ☐

- ☐

- ☐

Needs doing
- ☐

- ☐

- ☐

Low Priority
- ☐

- ☐

Action Plan

6am	
7am	
8am	
9am	
10am	
11am	
12pm	
1pm	
2pm	
3pm	
4pm	
5pm	
6pm	
7pm	
8pm	

Today I Feel

I deal with challenges by

I have the power to

What went well today?

What could have gone better?

What will tomorrow bring for you?

Ideas, Thoughts and Doodles

Date:_____

Daily Positive Thought

Daily Goal

To-Do List

Top Priority

❑

❑

❑

Needs doing

❑

❑

❑

Low Priority

❑

❑

Action Plan

6am	
7am	
8am	
9am	
10am	
11am	
12pm	
1pm	
2pm	
3pm	
4pm	
5pm	
6pm	
7pm	
8pm	

Today I Feel

I have the power to

I deal with challenges by

What went well today?

What could have gone better?

What will tomorrow bring for you?

Ideas, Thoughts and Doodles

Date:_____

Daily Positive Thought

Daily Goal

_____

_____

Action Plan

6am	
7am	
8am	
9am	
10am	
11am	
12pm	
1pm	
2pm	
3pm	
4pm	
5pm	
6pm	
7pm	
8pm	

To-Do List

Top Priority

❑

❑

❑

Needs doing

❑

❑

❑

Low Priority

❑

❑

Today I Feel

I deal with challenges by

I have the power to

What went well today?

What could have gone better?

What will tomorrow bring for you?

Ideas, Thoughts and Doodles

Date:_____

Daily Positive Thought

_____
_____

Daily Goal

To-Do List

Top Priority

☐

☐

☐

Needs doing

☐

☐

☐

Low Priority

☐

☐

Action Plan

6am	
7am	
8am	
9am	
10am	
11am	
12pm	
1pm	
2pm	
3pm	
4pm	
5pm	
6pm	
7pm	
8pm	

Today I Feel

I deal with challenges by

I have the power to

What went well today?

What could have gone better?

What will tomorrow bring for you?

Ideas, Thoughts and Doodles

Date:_____

Daily Positive Thought

_____
_____
_____

Daily Goal

To-Do List

Top Priority

☐

☐

☐

Needs doing

☐

☐

☐

Low Priority

☐

☐

Action Plan

6am

7am

8am

9am

10am

11am

12pm

1pm

2pm

3pm

4pm

5pm

6pm

7pm

8pm

Today I Feel

I deal with challenges by

I have the power to

What went well today?

What could have gone better?

What will tomorrow bring for you?

Ideas, Thoughts and Doodles

Date:_____

Daily Positive Thought

_____
_____
_____

Daily Goal

Action Plan

6am

7am

8am

9am

10am

11am

12pm

To-Do List

Top Priority

☐

☐

☐

Needs doing

☐

☐

☐

Low Priority

☐

☐

1pm

2pm

3pm

4pm

5pm

6pm

7pm

8pm

Today I Feel

I deal with challenges by

I have the power to

What went well today?

What could have gone better?

What will tomorrow bring for you?

Ideas, Thoughts and Doodles

Date:_____

Daily Positive Thought

_____
_____
_____

Daily Goal

To-Do List

Top Priority

☐

☐

☐

Needs doing

☐

☐

☐

Low Priority

☐

☐

Action Plan

6am	
7am	
8am	
9am	
10am	
11am	
12pm	
1pm	
2pm	
3pm	
4pm	
5pm	
6pm	
7pm	
8pm	

Today I Feel

I have the power to

I deal with challenges by

What went well today?

What could have gone better?

What will tomorrow bring for you?

Ideas, Thoughts and Doodles

Date:_____

Daily Positive Thought

Daily Goal

_____
_____

Action Plan

To-Do List

Top Priority

- ☐
- ☐
- ☐

Needs doing

- ☐
- ☐
- ☐

Low Priority

- ☐
- ☐

6am	
7am	
8am	
9am	
10am	
11am	
12pm	
1pm	
2pm	
3pm	
4pm	
5pm	
6pm	
7pm	
8pm	

Today I Feel

I deal with challenges by

I have the power to

What went well today?

What could have gone better?

What will tomorrow bring for you?

Ideas, Thoughts and Doodles

Date:_____

Daily Positive Thought

_____

_____

_____

Daily Goal

To-Do List

Top Priority

☐

☐

☐

Needs doing

☐

☐

☐

Low Priority

☐

☐

Action Plan

6am	
7am	
8am	
9am	
10am	
11am	
12pm	
1pm	
2pm	
3pm	
4pm	
5pm	
6pm	
7pm	
8pm	

Today I Feel

I deal with challenges by

I have the power to

What went well today?

What could have gone better?

What will tomorrow bring for you?

Ideas, Thoughts and Doodles

Date:_____

Daily Positive Thought

_____

_____

Daily Goal

To-Do List

Top Priority

☐

☐

☐

Needs doing

☐

☐

☐

Low Priority

☐

☐

Action Plan

6am	
7am	
8am	
9am	
10am	
11am	
12pm	
1pm	
2pm	
3pm	
4pm	
5pm	
6pm	
7pm	
8pm	

Today I Feel

I deal with challenges by

I have the power to

What went well today?

What could have gone better?

What will tomorrow bring for you?

Ideas, Thoughts and Doodles

Date:_____

Daily Positive Thought

Daily Goal

To-Do List

Top Priority

☐

☐

☐

Needs doing

☐

☐

☐

Low Priority

☐

☐

Today I Feel

I have the power to

Action Plan

6am	
7am	
8am	
9am	
10am	
11am	
12pm	
1pm	
2pm	
3pm	
4pm	
5pm	
6pm	
7pm	
8pm	

I deal with challenges by

What went well today?

What could have gone better?

What will tomorrow bring for you?

Ideas, Thoughts and Doodles

Date:_____

Daily Positive Thought

_____
_____

Daily Goal

To-Do List

Top Priority
- ☐
- ☐
- ☐

Needs doing
- ☐
- ☐
- ☐

Low Priority
- ☐
- ☐

Action Plan

6am	
7am	
8am	
9am	
10am	
11am	
12pm	
1pm	
2pm	
3pm	
4pm	
5pm	
6pm	
7pm	
8pm	

Today I Feel

I have the power to

I deal with challenges by

What went well today?

What could have gone better?

What will tomorrow bring for you?

Ideas, Thoughts and Doodles

Date:_____

Daily Positive Thought

Daily Goal

To-Do List

Top Priority

☐

☐

☐

Needs doing

☐

☐

☐

Low Priority

☐

☐

Action Plan

6am	
7am	
8am	
9am	
10am	
11am	
12pm	
1pm	
2pm	
3pm	
4pm	
5pm	
6pm	
7pm	
8pm	

Today I Feel

I have the power to

I deal with challenges by

What went well today?

What could have gone better?

What will tomorrow bring for you?

Ideas, Thoughts and Doodles

Date:_____

Daily Positive Thought

_____

_____

Daily Goal

To-Do List

Top Priority

☐

☐

☐

Needs doing

☐

☐

☐

Low Priority

☐

☐

Action Plan

6am	
7am	
8am	
9am	
10am	
11am	
12pm	
1pm	
2pm	
3pm	
4pm	
5pm	
6pm	
7pm	
8pm	

Today I Feel

I deal with challenges by

I have the power to

What went well today?

What could have gone better?

What will tomorrow bring for you?

Ideas, Thoughts and Doodles

Date:_____

Daily Positive Thought

_____
_____
_____

Daily Goal

Action Plan

6am	
7am	
8am	
9am	
10am	
11am	
12pm	
1pm	
2pm	
3pm	
4pm	
5pm	
6pm	
7pm	
8pm	

To-Do List

Top Priority
❑

❑

❑

Needs doing
❑

❑

❑

Low Priority
❑

❑

Today I Feel

I deal with challenges by

I have the power to

What went well today?

What could have gone better?

What will tomorrow bring for you?

Ideas, Thoughts and Doodles

Date:_____

Daily Positive Thought

_____

_____

Daily Goal

Action Plan

6am

7am

8am

9am

10am

11am

12pm

1pm

2pm

3pm

4pm

5pm

6pm

7pm

8pm

To-Do List

Top Priority

❑

❑

❑

Needs doing

❑

❑

❑

Low Priority

❑

❑

Today I Feel

I deal with challenges by

I have the power to

What went well today?

What could have gone better?

What will tomorrow bring for you?

Ideas, Thoughts and Doodles

Date:_____

Daily Positive Thought

_____

_____

Daily Goal

To-Do List

Top Priority

❑

❑

❑

Needs doing

❑

❑

❑

Low Priority

❑

❑

Action Plan

6am	
7am	
8am	
9am	
10am	
11am	
12pm	
1pm	
2pm	
3pm	
4pm	
5pm	
6pm	
7pm	
8pm	

Today I Feel

I have the power to

I deal with challenges by

What went well today?

What could have gone better?

What will tomorrow bring for you?

Ideas, Thoughts and Doodles

Date:_____   Daily Positive Thought

_____

Daily Goal

To-Do List

Top Priority

❑

❑

❑

Needs doing

❑

❑

❑

Low Priority

❑

❑

Today I Feel

I have the power to

Action Plan

6am
7am
8am
9am
10am
11am
12pm
1pm
2pm
3pm
4pm
5pm
6pm
7pm
8pm

I deal with challenges by

What went well today?

What could have gone better?

What will tomorrow bring for you?

Ideas, Thoughts and Doodles

Date:_____

Daily Positive Thought

_____

_____

Daily Goal

Action Plan

6am	
7am	
8am	
9am	
10am	
11am	
12pm	
1pm	
2pm	
3pm	
4pm	
5pm	
6pm	
7pm	
8pm	

To-Do List

Top Priority

☐

☐

☐

Needs doing

☐

☐

☐

Low Priority

☐

☐

Today I Feel

I deal with challenges by

I have the power to

What went well today?

What could have gone better?

What will tomorrow bring for you?

Ideas, Thoughts and Doodles

Date:_____

Daily Positive Thought

_____

_____

Daily Goal

To-Do List

Top Priority

❑

❑

❑

Needs doing

❑

❑

❑

Low Priority

❑

❑

Action Plan

6am	
7am	
8am	
9am	
10am	
11am	
12pm	
1pm	
2pm	
3pm	
4pm	
5pm	
6pm	
7pm	
8pm	

Today I Feel

I have the power to

I deal with challenges by

What went well today?

What could have gone better?

What will tomorrow bring for you?

Ideas, Thoughts and Doodles

Date:_____

Daily Positive Thought

_____

_____

Daily Goal

To-Do List

Top Priority

☐

☐

☐

Needs doing

☐

☐

☐

Low Priority

☐

☐

Action Plan

6am	
7am	
8am	
9am	
10am	
11am	
12pm	
1pm	
2pm	
3pm	
4pm	
5pm	
6pm	
7pm	
8pm	

Today I Feel

I deal with challenges by

I have the power to

What went well today?

What could have gone better?

What will tomorrow bring for you?

Ideas, Thoughts and Doodles

Date:_____

Daily Positive Thought
_____
_____

Daily Goal

To-Do List

Top Priority

☐

☐

☐

Needs doing

☐

☐

☐

Low Priority

☐

☐

Action Plan

6am	
7am	
8am	
9am	
10am	
11am	
12pm	
1pm	
2pm	
3pm	
4pm	
5pm	
6pm	
7pm	
8pm	

Today I Feel

I have the power to

I deal with challenges by

What went well today?

What could have gone better?

What will tomorrow bring for you?

Ideas, Thoughts and Doodles

Date:_____   Daily Positive Thought

Daily Goal

_____
_____
_____

Action Plan

6am	
7am	
8am	
9am	
10am	
11am	
12pm	
1pm	
2pm	
3pm	
4pm	
5pm	
6pm	
7pm	
8pm	

To-Do List

Top Priority

☐

☐

☐

Needs doing

☐

☐

☐

Low Priority

☐

☐

Today I Feel

I deal with challenges by

I have the power to

What went well today?

What could have gone better?

What will tomorrow bring for you?

Ideas, Thoughts and Doodles

Date:_____

Daily Positive Thought

_____

_____

Daily Goal

To-Do List

Action Plan

6am	
7am	
8am	
9am	
10am	
11am	
12pm	
1pm	
2pm	
3pm	
4pm	
5pm	
6pm	
7pm	
8pm	

Top Priority

❏

❏

❏

Needs doing

❏

❏

❏

Low Priority

❏

❏

Today I Feel

I deal with challenges by

I have the power to

What went well today?

What could have gone better?

What will tomorrow bring for you?

Ideas, Thoughts and Doodles

Date:_____

Daily Positive Thought

_____

_____

Daily Goal

To-Do List

Top Priority

❏

❏

❏

Needs doing

❏

❏

❏

Low Priority

❏

❏

Action Plan

6am	
7am	
8am	
9am	
10am	
11am	
12pm	
1pm	
2pm	
3pm	
4pm	
5pm	
6pm	
7pm	
8pm	

Today I Feel

I have the power to

I deal with challenges by

What went well today?

What could have gone better?

What will tomorrow bring for you?

Ideas, Thoughts and Doodles

Date:_____

Daily Positive Thought

_____

_____

Daily Goal

To-Do List

Top Priority

☐

☐

☐

Needs doing

☐

☐

☐

Low Priority

☐

☐

Action Plan

6am	
7am	
8am	
9am	
10am	
11am	
12pm	
1pm	
2pm	
3pm	
4pm	
5pm	
6pm	
7pm	
8pm	

Today I Feel

I have the power to

I deal with challenges by

What went well today?

What could have gone better?

What will tomorrow bring for you?

Ideas, Thoughts and Doodles

Date:_____

Daily Positive Thought

Daily Goal

To-Do List

Top Priority

❑

❑

❑

Needs doing

❑

❑

❑

Low Priority

❑

❑

Action Plan

6am	
7am	
8am	
9am	
10am	
11am	
12pm	
1pm	
2pm	
3pm	
4pm	
5pm	
6pm	
7pm	
8pm	

Today I Feel

I have the power to

I deal with challenges by

What went well today?

What could have gone better?

What will tomorrow bring for you?

Ideas, Thoughts and Doodles

Date:_____

Daily Positive Thought

_____

_____

Daily Goal

Action Plan

6am	
7am	
8am	
9am	
10am	
11am	
12pm	
1pm	
2pm	
3pm	
4pm	
5pm	
6pm	
7pm	
8pm	

To-Do List

Top Priority
- ☐
- ☐
- ☐

Needs doing
- ☐
- ☐
- ☐

Low Priority
- ☐
- ☐

Today I Feel

I deal with challenges by

I have the power to

What went well today?

What could have gone better?

What will tomorrow bring for you?

Ideas, Thoughts and Doodles

Date:_____

Daily Positive Thought

_____

_____

Daily Goal

To-Do List

Top Priority

❑

❑

❑

Needs doing

❑

❑

❑

Low Priority

❑

❑

Action Plan

6am	
7am	
8am	
9am	
10am	
11am	
12pm	
1pm	
2pm	
3pm	
4pm	
5pm	
6pm	
7pm	
8pm	

Today I Feel

I have the power to

I deal with challenges by

What went well today?

What could have gone better?

What will tomorrow bring for you?

Ideas, Thoughts and Doodles

Date:_____   Daily Positive Thought
                              _____

Daily Goal   _____

Action Plan

6am	
7am	
8am	
## To-Do List	9am	
10am	
Top Priority	11am	
☐	12pm	
1pm	
☐	2pm	
3pm	
☐	4pm	
5pm	
Needs doing	6pm	
☐	7pm	
8pm	
☐

☐

Low Priority
☐

☐

Today I Feel   ## I deal with challenges by

I have the power to

What went well today?

What could have gone better?

What will tomorrow bring for you?

Ideas, Thoughts and Doodles

Date:_____

Daily Positive Thought

_____

_____

Daily Goal

Action Plan

6am	
7am	
8am	
9am	
10am	
11am	
12pm	
1pm	
2pm	
3pm	
4pm	
5pm	
6pm	
7pm	
8pm	

To-Do List

Top Priority

❑

❑

❑

Needs doing

❑

❑

❑

Low Priority

❑

❑

Today I Feel

I deal with challenges by

I have the power to

What went well today?

What could have gone better?

What will tomorrow bring for you?

Ideas, Thoughts and Doodles

Date:_____

Daily Positive Thought

_____
_____

Daily Goal

To-Do List

Top Priority

☐

☐

☐

Needs doing

☐

☐

☐

Low Priority

☐

☐

Action Plan

6am	
7am	
8am	
9am	
10am	
11am	
12pm	
1pm	
2pm	
3pm	
4pm	
5pm	
6pm	
7pm	
8pm	

Today I Feel

I have the power to

I deal with challenges by

What went well today?

What could have gone better?

What will tomorrow bring for you?

Ideas, Thoughts and Doodles

Date:_____

Daily Positive Thought

_____

Daily Goal

To-Do List

Top Priority

☐

☐

☐

Needs doing

☐

☐

☐

Low Priority

☐

☐

Action Plan

| 6am |
| 7am |
| 8am |
| 9am |
| 10am |
| 11am |
| 12pm |
| 1pm |
| 2pm |
| 3pm |
| 4pm |
| 5pm |
| 6pm |
| 7pm |
| 8pm |

Today I Feel

I deal with challenges by

I have the power to

What went well today?

What could have gone better?

What will tomorrow bring for you?

Ideas, Thoughts and Doodles

Date:_____

Daily Positive Thought

_____

_____

Daily Goal

Action Plan

6am	
7am	
8am	
9am	
10am	
11am	
12pm	
1pm	
2pm	
3pm	
4pm	
5pm	
6pm	
7pm	
8pm	

To-Do List

Top Priority

❑

❑

❑

Needs doing

❑

❑

❑

Low Priority

❑

❑

Today I Feel

I deal with challenges by

I have the power to

What went well today?

What could have gone better?

What will tomorrow bring for you?

Ideas, Thoughts and Doodles

Date:_____

Daily Positive Thought

_____

_____

Daily Goal

To-Do List

Top Priority
- ❏
- ❏
- ❏

Needs doing
- ❏
- ❏
- ❏

Low Priority
- ❏
- ❏

Action Plan

6am	
7am	
8am	
9am	
10am	
11am	
12pm	
1pm	
2pm	
3pm	
4pm	
5pm	
6pm	
7pm	
8pm	

Today I Feel

I have the power to

I deal with challenges by

What went well today?

What could have gone better?

What will tomorrow bring for you?

Ideas, Thoughts and Doodles

Date:_____

Daily Positive Thought

_____

_____

Daily Goal

To-Do List

Top Priority

❑

❑

❑

Needs doing

❑

❑

❑

Low Priority

❑

❑

Action Plan

6am	
7am	
8am	
9am	
10am	
11am	
12pm	
1pm	
2pm	
3pm	
4pm	
5pm	
6pm	
7pm	
8pm	

Today I Feel

I have the power to

I deal with challenges by

What went well today?

What could have gone better?

What will tomorrow bring for you?

Ideas, Thoughts and Doodles

Date:_____   # Daily Positive Thought

Daily Goal

_____

_____

Action Plan

6am	
7am	
8am	
9am	
10am	
11am	
12pm	
1pm	
2pm	
3pm	
4pm	
5pm	
6pm	
7pm	
8pm	

To-Do List

Top Priority

❑

❑

❑

Needs doing

❑

❑

❑

Low Priority

❑

❑

Today I Feel

I have the power to

I deal with challenges by

What went well today?

What could have gone better?

What will tomorrow bring for you?

Ideas, Thoughts and Doodles

Date:_____

Daily Positive Thought

_____

_____

Daily Goal

To-Do List

Top Priority

❑

❑

❑

Needs doing

❑

❑

❑

Low Priority

❑

❑

Action Plan

6am	
7am	
8am	
9am	
10am	
11am	
12pm	
1pm	
2pm	
3pm	
4pm	
5pm	
6pm	
7pm	
8pm	

Today I Feel

I have the power to

I deal with challenges by

What went well today?

What could have gone better?

What will tomorrow bring for you?

Ideas, Thoughts and Doodles

Date:_____

Daily Positive Thought

Daily Goal

To-Do List

Top Priority

❑

❑

❑

Needs doing

❑

❑

❑

Low Priority

❑

❑

Action Plan

6am	
7am	
8am	
9am	
10am	
11am	
12pm	
1pm	
2pm	
3pm	
4pm	
5pm	
6pm	
7pm	
8pm	

Today I Feel

I have the power to

I deal with challenges by

What went well today?

What could have gone better?

What will tomorrow bring for you?

Ideas, Thoughts and Doodles

Date:_____

Daily Positive Thought

_____

_____

Daily Goal

To-Do List

Top Priority

❑

❑

❑

Needs doing

❑

❑

❑

Low Priority

❑

❑

Action Plan

| 6am |
| 7am |
| 8am |
| 9am |
| 10am |
| 11am |
| 12pm |
| 1pm |
| 2pm |
| 3pm |
| 4pm |
| 5pm |
| 6pm |
| 7pm |
| 8pm |

Today I Feel

I deal with challenges by

I have the power to

What went well today?

What could have gone better?

What will tomorrow bring for you?

Ideas, Thoughts and Doodles

Date:_____ Daily Positive Thought

_____

Daily Goal

_____

Action Plan

6am	
7am	
8am	
9am	
10am	
11am	
12pm	
1pm	
2pm	
3pm	
4pm	
5pm	
6pm	
7pm	
8pm	

To-Do List

Top Priority
❑

❑

❑

Needs doing
❑

❑

❑

Low Priority
❑

❑

Today I Feel

I deal with challenges by

I have the power to

What went well today?

What could have gone better?

What will tomorrow bring for you?

Ideas, Thoughts and Doodles

Date:_____

Daily Positive Thought

_____

_____

Daily Goal

To-Do List

Top Priority

❑

❑

❑

Needs doing

❑

❑

❑

Low Priority

❑

❑

Action Plan

6am
7am
8am
9am
10am
11am
12pm
1pm
2pm
3pm
4pm
5pm
6pm
7pm
8pm

Today I Feel

I deal with challenges by

I have the power to

What went well today?

What could have gone better?

What will tomorrow bring for you?

Ideas, Thoughts and Doodles

Date:_____

Daily Positive Thought

_____

_____

Daily Goal

To-Do List

Top Priority

❑

❑

❑

Needs doing

❑

❑

❑

Low Priority

❑

❑

Action Plan

6am	
7am	
8am	
9am	
10am	
11am	
12pm	
1pm	
2pm	
3pm	
4pm	
5pm	
6pm	
7pm	
8pm	

Today I Feel

I have the power to

I deal with challenges by

What went well today?

What could have gone better?

What will tomorrow bring for you?

Ideas, Thoughts and Doodles

Date:_____

Daily Positive Thought

_____
_____
_____

Daily Goal

Action Plan

6am

7am

8am

9am

10am

11am

12pm

1pm

2pm

3pm

4pm

5pm

6pm

7pm

8pm

To-Do List

Top Priority

❑

❑

❑

Needs doing

❑

❑

❑

Low Priority

❑

❑

Today I Feel

I deal with challenges by

I have the power to

What went well today?

What could have gone better?

What will tomorrow bring for you?

Ideas, Thoughts and Doodles

Date:_____

Daily Positive Thought

_____

_____

Daily Goal

To-Do List

Top Priority

☐

☐

☐

Needs doing

☐

☐

☐

Low Priority

☐

☐

Action Plan

6am	
7am	
8am	
9am	
10am	
11am	
12pm	
1pm	
2pm	
3pm	
4pm	
5pm	
6pm	
7pm	
8pm	

Today I Feel

I have the power to

I deal with challenges by

What went well today?

What could have gone better?

What will tomorrow bring for you?

Ideas, Thoughts and Doodles

Date:_____   # Daily Positive Thought

Daily Goal

_____

_____

To-Do List

Top Priority

❑

❑

❑

Needs doing

❑

❑

❑

Low Priority

❑

❑

Action Plan

| 6am |
| 7am |
| 8am |
| 9am |
| 10am |
| 11am |
| 12pm |
| 1pm |
| 2pm |
| 3pm |
| 4pm |
| 5pm |
| 6pm |
| 7pm |
| 8pm |

Today I Feel

I deal with challenges by

I have the power to

What went well today?

What could have gone better?

What will tomorrow bring for you?

Ideas, Thoughts and Doodles

Date:_____

Daily Positive Thought

Daily Goal

To-Do List

Top Priority

❑

❑

❑

Needs doing

❑

❑

❑

Low Priority

❑

❑

Action Plan

6am	
7am	
8am	
9am	
10am	
11am	
12pm	
1pm	
2pm	
3pm	
4pm	
5pm	
6pm	
7pm	
8pm	

Today I Feel

I have the power to

I deal with challenges by

What went well today?

What could have gone better?

What will tomorrow bring for you?

Ideas, Thoughts and Doodles

Date:_____   Daily Positive Thought

Daily Goal

To-Do List

Top Priority
☐

☐

☐

Needs doing
☐

☐

☐

Low Priority
☐

☐

Today I Feel

I have the power to

_____

_____

Action Plan

6am	
7am	
8am	
9am	
10am	
11am	
12pm	
1pm	
2pm	
3pm	
4pm	
5pm	
6pm	
7pm	
8pm	

I deal with challenges by

What went well today?

What could have gone better?

What will tomorrow bring for you?

Ideas, Thoughts and Doodles

Date:_____ Daily Positive Thought

Daily Goal

To-Do List

Top Priority
❑

❑

❑

Needs doing
❑

❑

❑

Low Priority
❑

❑

Today I Feel

I have the power to

_____

_____

Action Plan

6am

7am

8am

9am

10am

11am

12pm

1pm

2pm

3pm

4pm

5pm

6pm

7pm

8pm

I deal with challenges by

What went well today?

What could have gone better?

What will tomorrow bring for you?

Ideas, Thoughts and Doodles

Date:_____

Daily Positive Thought

_____
_____
_____

Daily Goal

To-Do List

Top Priority

☐

☐

☐

Needs doing

☐

☐

☐

Low Priority

☐

☐

Action Plan

6am	
7am	
8am	
9am	
10am	
11am	
12pm	
1pm	
2pm	
3pm	
4pm	
5pm	
6pm	
7pm	
8pm	

Today I Feel

I have the power to

I deal with challenges by

What went well today?

What could have gone better?

What will tomorrow bring for you?

Ideas, Thoughts and Doodles

Date:_____   Daily Positive Thought

Daily Goal

To-Do List

Top Priority

❑

❑

❑

Needs doing

❑

❑

❑

Low Priority

❑

❑

Today I Feel

I have the power to

Action Plan

6am

7am

8am

9am

10am

11am

12pm

1pm

2pm

3pm

4pm

5pm

6pm

7pm

8pm

I deal with challenges by

What went well today?

What could have gone better?

What will tomorrow bring for you?

Ideas, Thoughts and Doodles

Date:_____   Daily Positive Thought

Daily Goal

_____

_____

Action Plan

6am	
7am	
8am	
9am	
10am	
11am	
12pm	
1pm	
2pm	
3pm	
4pm	
5pm	
6pm	
7pm	
8pm	

To-Do List

Top Priority
☐

☐

☐

Needs doing
☐

☐

☐

Low Priority
☐

☐

Today I Feel

I deal with challenges by

I have the power to

What went well today?

What could have gone better?

What will tomorrow bring for you?

Ideas, Thoughts and Doodles

Date:_____

Daily Positive Thought

_____

_____

Daily Goal

To-Do List

Top Priority

☐

☐

☐

Needs doing

☐

☐

☐

Low Priority

☐

☐

Action Plan

6am	
7am	
8am	
9am	
10am	
11am	
12pm	
1pm	
2pm	
3pm	
4pm	
5pm	
6pm	
7pm	
8pm	

Today I Feel

I have the power to

I deal with challenges by

What went well today?

What could have gone better?

What will tomorrow bring for you?

Ideas, Thoughts and Doodles

Date:_____   Daily Positive Thought

Daily Goal

To-Do List

Top Priority

❑

❑

❑

Needs doing

❑

❑

❑

Low Priority

❑

❑

Today I Feel

I have the power to

_____

_____

Action Plan

| 6am |
| 7am |
| 8am |
| 9am |
| 10am |
| 11am |
| 12pm |
| 1pm |
| 2pm |
| 3pm |
| 4pm |
| 5pm |
| 6pm |
| 7pm |
| 8pm |

I deal with challenges by

What went well today?

What could have gone better?

What will tomorrow bring for you?

Ideas, Thoughts and Doodles

Date:_____

Daily Positive Thought

Daily Goal

_____
_____

Action Plan

6am	
7am	
8am	
9am	
10am	
11am	
12pm	
1pm	
2pm	
3pm	
4pm	
5pm	
6pm	
7pm	
8pm	

To-Do List

Top Priority
- ☐
- ☐
- ☐

Needs doing
- ☐
- ☐
- ☐

Low Priority
- ☐
- ☐

Today I Feel

I have the power to

I deal with challenges by

What went well today?

What could have gone better?

What will tomorrow bring for you?

Ideas, Thoughts and Doodles

Date:_____   # Daily Positive Thought

Daily Goal

_____

_____

Action Plan

To-Do List	
Top Priority	6am
☐	7am
	8am
☐	9am
	10am
☐	11am
Needs doing	12pm
☐	1pm
	2pm
☐	3pm
	4pm
☐	5pm
Low Priority	6pm
☐	7pm
	8pm
☐	

Today I Feel

I deal with challenges by

I have the power to

What went well today?

What could have gone better?

What will tomorrow bring for you?

Ideas, Thoughts and Doodles

Date:_____

Daily Positive Thought

_____
_____

Daily Goal

Action Plan

6am	
7am	
8am	
9am	
10am	
11am	
12pm	
1pm	
2pm	
3pm	
4pm	
5pm	
6pm	
7pm	
8pm	

To-Do List

Top Priority

❑

❑

❑

Needs doing

❑

❑

❑

Low Priority

❑

❑

Today I Feel

I deal with challenges by

I have the power to